UNSHACKLING FROM APPROVAL AND REJECTION

A Journey to Self-Empowerment

Oreoluwa O. Olaleye

Fused-Up Innovations

To all the brave souls who have struggled with seeking approval and fearing rejection, may this book be a guiding light on your journey to self-empowerment.

To those who have felt the weight of societal expectations, and to those who have grappled with self-doubt, this book is dedicated to you.

To the ones who have dared to break free from the chains of external validation and to embrace their true selves, your courage is an inspiration.

To my friends, family, and loved ones who have supported me in this endeavor, thank you for always believing in me.

And finally, to myself - for having the courage to explore the depths of human emotions and for embarking on a quest to understand the complexities of seeking approval and fearing rejection. May this book serve as a reminder of my own journey towards self-discovery and self-acceptance.

This book is for all of you, with love and gratitude. May it spark a revolution of self-empowerment and liberation, one reader at a time.

In the quest for approval, we may find fleeting comfort, but in embracing our authenticity despite rejection, we discover the true essence of self-empowerment.

OREOLUWA O. OLALEYE

CONTENTS

INTRODUCTION

Ladies and gentlemen, aliens, and beings of all shapes and sizes, gather 'round, for I have an epic tale to share with you today! Picture this: a world where seeking approval is as common as the daily coffee run, and fearing rejection is like facing a swarm of angry bees armed with nothing but a fly swatter. It's a rollercoaster of emotions, my friends, and we're about to take a wild ride through the hilariously tangled web of human behavior!

Ah, yes, welcome to a place where seeking external validation has become a sport more popular than any Olympic event. We're talking about a world where people aren't just content with their own opinions; they need the stamp of approval from the entire universe before they feel validated. I mean, come on, who needs self-confidence when you have an army of "likes" and "thumbs up" at your disposal?

And then, there's the flip side, my dear adventurers. The fear of rejection lurks in the shadows like a mischievous gremlin, ready to pounce at the slightest hint of vulnerability. It's like walking through a field of landmines, trying to avoid anything that might dent our fragile egos. Oh, the lengths we go to escape the dreaded "no"!

But fear not, fellow explorers, for in this very book, "Unshackling from Approval and Rejection: A Journey to Self-Empowerment," we shall venture deep into the wilderness of validation-seeking and rejection sensitivity. Armed with laughter and wit, we'll unravel the mystery of why we humans just can't seem to get enough of external validation and why the fear of rejection lingers like the smell of burnt popcorn in a microwave.

Prepare yourselves for a thrilling adventure filled with quirky anecdotes, bizarre experiments, and maybe even a dance-off with the validation-seeking aliens from Planet Zog. Okay, maybe not the last part, but we'll keep it in mind for the sequel!

Together, we shall navigate the treacherous waters of low self-esteem and the siren call of approval. We'll uncover the roots of these peculiar behaviors, from childhood traumas to that one embarrassing moment at the company picnic that haunts our dreams. It's time to face our fears and embrace our quirks with open arms (and perhaps a dab of glitter, because why not?).

So fasten your seatbelts, my friends, and get ready to embark on a journey of self-discovery, laughter, and maybe a few cringe-worthy moments. Let's dive headfirst into the world of "Unshackling from Approval and Rejection: A Journey to Self-Empowerment." It's going to be a bumpy, enlightening, and hilariously heartwarming ride that will leave you saying, "Wow, I never thought my insecurities could be so entertaining!"

Oh, and don't forget to bring your sense of humor and a cozy blanket for those awkward moments when we cringe at our own human antics. Adventure awaits! Let's embark on this comical quest to understand the whimsical ways of our fellow earthlings and uncover the secrets of self-empowerment in the face of validation-seeking and rejection fears. Onward we go!

PROLOGUE

Once upon a time, in a world not so far away, where reality was stranger than fiction and humor ruled the land, there existed a curious bunch of humans. These were not your ordinary, run-of-the-mill humans; oh no, they were a bunch of quirky, slightly offbeat, and downright comical creatures who lived for the thrills of seeking approval and dodging rejection like they were navigating a never-ending game of emotional dodgeball.

But let me tell you, dear reader, this wasn't your typical fairy tale with knights in shining armor and damsels in distress. No, this was a tale of the absurd, where approval-seeking had become the national pastime, and rejection fears were more dramatic than any soap opera you've ever seen. It was as if the entire world had formed an intricate dance, where everyone tried to outdo each other in the "Look How Perfect My Life Is" competition.

In this comically chaotic world, we find our heroes, Adamu and Evian, two best friends who couldn't be more different if they tried. Adamu was the quintessential validation seeker, constantly seeking approval from everyone and their grandmother. If he posted a selfie on social media and didn't receive enough likes, you'd think the sky was falling.

On the other hand, we had Evian, a self-proclaimed "rejection warrior," who would go to incredible lengths to avoid anything that could potentially result in rejection. From avoiding job interviews like the plague to turning down blind dates with the enthusiasm of a toddler facing broccoli, Evian was the master of evasion.

As fate would have it, these two lovable misfits found themselves on an adventure of a lifetime, as they stumbled upon an ancient artifact known as the "Mirror of Truth." Rumor had it that this magical mirror had the power to reveal the deepest secrets of one's soul and liberate them from the shackles of approval-seeking and rejection fears.

With equal parts excitement and trepidation, Adamu and Evian embarked on a journey to unlock the mirror's powers, hoping to find the courage to be their authentic selves and break free from the absurd pressures of society. Along the way, they encountered a motley crew of characters – from an eccentric life coach with an affinity for puns to a wise old owl who spoke only in riddles.

As our intrepid duo delved deeper into the labyrinth of emotions, they discovered that seeking approval and fearing rejection were not as black and white as they seemed. It was a messy, hilarious, and at times, heartwarming exploration of what it truly means to be human.

Through laughter, tears, and plenty of witty banter, Adamu and Evian learned that the path to self-empowerment was not about living for the approval of others or running away from rejection. It was about embracing their quirks, celebrating their imperfections, and finding the courage to be authentically themselves – even if it meant making a few blunders along the way.

So, dear reader, buckle up for a sidesplitting, heartwarming adventure as we dive headfirst into the comical world of Adamu and Evian, where seeking validation and fearing rejection collide in a cosmic explosion of hilarity and self-discovery. Get ready to laugh, gasp, and maybe even shed a tear or two, as we unveil the absurdity and beauty of the human experience.

* * *

A Journey to Self-Empowerment

THE HABIT OF SEEKING APPROVAL

We begin by exploring the pervasive habit of seeking approval from others, understanding how it can subtly infiltrate our lives. From relying on external validation to suppressing our authentic desires, we examine the various manifestations of this behavior and its impact on our well-being.

The habit of seeking approval is a common behavioral pattern in which individuals look to others for validation, acceptance, and recognition of their thoughts, actions, and decisions. It involves seeking external confirmation and permission from others before proceeding with personal choices and actions. People who develop this habit often prioritize the opinions and approval of others over their own internal values and desires.

This behavior can manifest in various ways in everyday life, including:

Seeking constant reassurance:
Individuals who seek approval may constantly seek reassurance from others about their appearance, abilities, or decisions. They may ask for feedback and validation on even minor tasks or choices.

Fear of disapproval:
People with a strong habit of seeking approval may have an intense fear of rejection or disapproval from others. This fear can be so overwhelming that it affects their ability to make independent decisions.

Over-explaining:
Those seeking approval may find themselves over-explaining their choices and actions to others, hoping to gain acceptance and understanding.

Difficulty saying "no":
People with this habit may have difficulty saying

"no" to others, even when it is inconvenient or against their own interests, to avoid disappointing or upsetting others.

Dependency on external validation:
Seeking approval becomes a way of validating one's self-worth and confidence, making individuals dependent on others' opinions to feel good about themselves.

The Habit of Seeking Approval and Self-Esteem:

The habit of seeking approval is often linked to self-esteem issues. People who lack self-confidence and have low self-esteem may seek external validation as a way to feel accepted and valued. They may believe that their worth is dependent on others' opinions and validation, leading to a perpetual cycle of seeking approval.

Root Causes:
The habit of seeking approval can be rooted in various factors, including:

Childhood upbringing:

Early experiences and upbringing can significantly influence the development of this habit. Children who grew up in environments where their actions were constantly scrutinized or criticized may internalize the need for constant approval.

Fear of rejection:

Past experiences of rejection or disapproval can lead individuals to seek approval as a defense mechanism to avoid similar negative experiences in the future.

Need for belongingness:

Humans are social beings, and the need for belongingness and acceptance is natural. However, when this need becomes excessive, it can lead to the habit of seeking approval.

Impact on Decision-Making and Autonomy:

The habit of seeking approval can significantly impact decision-making and autonomy. People who constantly seek approval from others may find themselves unable to make independent choices and rely heavily on external guidance. This can limit personal growth and prevent individuals from exploring their true passions and desires.

Breaking the Habit:

Breaking the habit of seeking approval requires self-awareness, self-reflection, and a willingness to change. Here are some strategies to overcome this habit:

Build self-confidence:

Focus on building self-confidence and self-esteem by recognizing your strengths, accomplishments, and unique qualities.

Trust your instincts:

Learn to trust your instincts and intuition when making decisions instead of constantly seeking validation from others.

Set boundaries:

Establish healthy boundaries and learn to say "no" when necessary. Understand that it's okay to prioritize your own well-being and needs.

Challenge negative thoughts:

Challenge negative thoughts and beliefs that may be contributing to the habit of seeking approval. Practice positive affirmations and self-compassion.

Seek internal validation:
Cultivate a sense of self-approval and self-validation. Acknowledge that your worth does not depend on others' opinions.

In Conclusion:
Breaking the habit of seeking approval is a journey of self-discovery and empowerment. By cultivating self-confidence and learning to trust your own judgment, you can reclaim control over your life and make decisions based on your authentic self, rather than seeking external validation. Embracing your uniqueness and individuality will lead to a more fulfilling and confident life.

A TALE OF SEEKING APPROVAL

Once upon a time in the vibrant city of Veritopia, there were two best friends named Adamu and Evian. They were inseparable, having known each other since childhood. Both Adamu and Evian had big dreams and aspirations, and they supported each other in every endeavor.

However, as they grew older, Adamu became increasingly preoccupied with seeking approval from others. He was a talented musician and dreamed of starting his own band, but he often doubted his abilities. Adamu would perform on street corners, hoping for the validation of passersby.

He craved applause and compliments, believing that they were the keys to his success.

On the other hand, Evian was a gifted artist with a flair for fashion design. She had an extraordinary vision for her creations but was hesitant to showcase her designs to the world. Evian would spend hours perfecting her sketches and stitching garments in her little studio, but she was afraid of criticism and rejection.

One sunny afternoon, Adamu and Evian decided to take a stroll through the bustling streets of Veritopia. As they meandered through the lively market, they stumbled upon a grand talent show being held in the town square. The event was bustling with performers, artists, and musicians, all vying for the approval of the judges and the enthusiastic crowd.

Adamu's eyes gleamed with excitement as he watched the performers captivate the audience with their talents. "Evian, this could be our chance! We should sign up and show the world what we can do!" he exclaimed, his heart pounding with anticipation.

Evian felt a twinge of nervousness but nodded in agreement. "You're right, Adamu. It's time to step out of our comfort zones and embrace our passions. Let's do it!"

With newfound determination, they registered for the talent show, Adamu with his guitar, and Evian with her exquisite collection of fashion designs. As the day of the event approached, they practiced tirelessly, encouraging each other to believe in themselves and their unique talents.

The day of the talent show arrived, and Veritopia's town square was bustling with excitement. Adamu and Evian were backstage, their hearts racing with a mix of nervousness and anticipation. "We've got this, Evian. Let's show them what we're made of!" Adamu said, giving Evian a reassuring smile.

First up was Adamu. He stepped onto the stage with his guitar, feeling a mixture of fear and excitement coursing through his veins. As he began to strum his guitar and sing from the depths of his soul, something magical happened. The audience fell silent, completely captivated by his raw talent and heartfelt lyrics. Applause erupted like thunder as he finished his performance, and tears of joy streamed down Adamu's cheeks.

Next was Evian's turn. She walked confidently onto the stage, showcasing her collection of avant-garde fashion designs. Each garment was a masterpiece, a reflection of her creative brilliance. As the models paraded down the runway, the crowd erupted into applause, mesmerized by Evian's extraordinary creations.

After the talent show, Adamu and Evian were overwhelmed with the outpouring of praise and admiration they received. Strangers approached them with glowing compliments, and the judges commended them on their exceptional talents. In that moment, they realized that seeking approval from others wasn't as gratifying as they thought; the real reward came from believing in themselves and pursuing their passions with authenticity.

As they walked home hand in hand that night, Adamu and Evian felt an unbreakable bond between them. They had learned that seeking approval from others would never fulfill them as much as the self-belief and genuine love for their crafts did. From that day on, they embraced their true selves, unapologetically pursuing their passions, and shining brightly in their own unique ways.

And so, dear reader, the tale of Adamu and Evian serves as a reminder that seeking approval from others may bring fleeting validation, but it is the unwavering self-confidence and self-belief that lead to true fulfillment and success. Let their story inspire you to embrace your passions, chase your dreams, and dance to the rhythm of your heart, for the world is waiting to applaud the beautiful masterpiece that is you.

THE FEAR OF REJECTION

Next, we turn our focus to rejection sensitivity and its profound effect on our decision-making and pursuit of opportunities. Discover the roots of this fear and how it can create a self-perpetuating cycle of avoidance and limited growth.

Rejection sensitivity is a psychological phenomenon characterized by an intense fear of rejection or negative evaluation from others. Individuals who experience rejection sensitivity are highly attuned to cues that may indicate possible rejection, criticism, or disapproval, even in situations where it may not be intended. This heightened sensitivity can significantly impact various aspects of their lives, including decision-making and pursuit of opportunities.

Key Characteristics Of Rejection Sensitivity:

Sensitivity to Social Cues:
People with rejection sensitivity are hypersensitive to social cues, body language, and verbal expressions that might suggest rejection or disapproval. They may interpret neutral or ambiguous feedback as negative, leading to heightened anxiety and self-doubt.

Overthinking and Catastrophizing:
Individuals with rejection sensitivity often engage in overthinking and catastrophizing scenarios in their minds. They may imagine worst-case outcomes, believing that rejection or failure is inevitable, which can lead to avoidance behavior.

Fear of Abandonment:
Rejection sensitivity is often linked to a fear of abandonment and a strong desire for acceptance and belongingness. The fear of losing relationships or opportunities can be overwhelming, leading to

anxious and defensive reactions.

Impact on Self-Esteem:
Rejection sensitivity can significantly impact self-esteem. Individuals may internalize perceived rejections as evidence of their inadequacy or unworthiness, leading to a negative self-concept and reduced self-confidence.

Effects On Decision-Making:

Rejection sensitivity can have several profound effects on decision-making:

Avoidance of Risks:
People with rejection sensitivity may avoid taking risks or pursuing opportunities that involve uncertainty. The fear of potential rejection or failure can lead them to stick to the familiar and safe, even if it means missing out on growth and development opportunities.

Hesitation in Relationships:
In personal relationships, individuals with rejection sensitivity may hesitate to express their feelings or needs. They may fear rejection and subsequently

refrain from initiating or deepening connections, leading to missed opportunities for meaningful relationships.

Professional Impact:

Rejection sensitivity can also impact professional decisions. Individuals may avoid seeking promotions, applying for competitive positions, or presenting new ideas at work due to a fear of rejection or negative evaluation.

Limiting Potential:

Ultimately, rejection sensitivity can limit an individual's potential for personal and professional growth. The constant need for validation and avoidance of potential rejection can prevent them from embracing challenges and fully exploring their abilities.

Overcoming Rejection Sensitivity:

Overcoming rejection sensitivity is a gradual and challenging process, but it is essential for personal and emotional well-being. Here are some strategies to address rejection sensitivity:

Cognitive Restructuring:

Challenge negative thought patterns and catastrophic thinking by questioning the evidence for potential rejection. Develop more balanced and realistic perspectives.

Emotion Regulation:

Learn to manage and regulate emotions associated with rejection sensitivity, such as anxiety and fear. Mindfulness and relaxation techniques can be helpful in reducing emotional reactivity.

Seek Social Support:

Talk to friends, family, or a therapist about your feelings of rejection sensitivity. Sharing your experiences and emotions with others can provide validation and a different perspective.

Behavioral Exposure:

Gradually expose yourself to situations that trigger rejection sensitivity in a controlled and supportive environment. This can help desensitize you to the fear of rejection and build resilience.

Self-Compassion:

Cultivate self-compassion and self-acceptance. Remind yourself that everyone experiences rejection and failure at times, and it does not define your worth as a person.

In Conclusion:

Rejection sensitivity can have a significant impact on decision-making and the pursuit of opportunities. The fear of rejection and negative evaluation can lead to avoidance behavior and limit personal and professional growth. Recognizing rejection sensitivity and taking steps to address it can lead to increased self-confidence, improved decision-making, and a more fulfilling life with a greater openness to pursuing opportunities and forming meaningful connections.

A TALE ON THE FEAR OF REJECTION

In the enchanting world of Veritopia, there lived two best friends, Adamu and Evian, who had always shared a deep fear of rejection. From a young age, they had experienced moments of criticism and disapproval that left lasting impressions on their tender hearts.

Adamu's fear of rejection stemmed from a childhood incident when he auditioned for a school play. Despite his passion for music and performing, he froze on stage when faced with a panel of judges and an audience. The waves of self-doubt had washed over him, leaving a lingering fear of judgment and rejection that he carried into adulthood.

Evian, too, had experienced her fair share of rejection. In school, she had presented one of her early fashion designs to her classmates, only to be met with giggles and teasing. The painful memory of that moment had instilled a deep fear of exposing her creative soul to the world, causing her to hide her talents away from others.

As the years passed, Adamu and Evian nurtured their friendship, finding solace in their shared fears. They found comfort in the familiar, in each other's company, where they could avoid the possibility of rejection from the outside world. The thought of putting themselves out there and facing judgment was far too daunting.

One day, as they sat in their favorite spot by the riverbank, a wise old storyteller named Amani approached them. Sensing their apprehension, she kindly smiled and said, "I've observed the two of you from afar. I sense that fear has taken root in your hearts. But remember, dear ones, the world is vast and ever-changing. It is in embracing change that we grow and evolve."

Adamu and Evian exchanged puzzled glances but were intrigued by the old woman's words. Amani continued, "Your fear of rejection is keeping you from discovering your true potential. Each of you has unique gifts that the world is waiting to receive, but you must have the courage to share them. Do not let fear hold you back from the wondrous possibilities life has to offer."

Her words struck a chord within them, and they couldn't help but reflect on their lives and the opportunities they had missed due to their fear of rejection. Amani sensed their inner turmoil and offered a small, leather-bound book.

"This is a book of possibilities," she said. "Write down all the dreams and desires you have buried deep inside due to fear. Face your fears head-on, and let the world witness the brilliance within you."

Adamu and Evian hesitated at first, their minds racing with doubts and insecurities. But slowly, they began to pen down their dreams, overcoming their inner resistance one word at a time.

Adamu dreamt of creating a band that could touch people's hearts with their music, while Evian envisioned her fashion designs gracing the runways of the world. Each page of the book became a testament to their hidden desires and untapped potential.

With newfound determination, they took their first steps towards realizing their dreams. Adamu gathered the courage to perform on street corners, receiving both praise and constructive feedback. Evian started showcasing her designs to a small circle of friends and family, learning to embrace both positive responses and critiques.

As they embraced their fears, they discovered the exhilaration of growth and self-discovery. The more they faced potential rejection, the stronger they became. Each experience, whether positive or not, brought valuable lessons that they incorporated into their crafts.

As the seasons changed, so did Adamu and Evian. They bloomed like flowers that had finally seen the sunlight after a long winter. Their talents, once hidden away, now radiated with confidence and authenticity. The world noticed their transformation, and soon, their passions began to touch the lives of others.

In time, Adamu's band became known for its heartfelt performances, and Evian's designs earned accolades for their creativity and ingenuity. They realized that the opinions of others, whether favorable or critical, did not define their worth. What mattered most was staying true to themselves and sharing their gifts with the world.

And so, dear reader, Adamu and Evian's tale reminds

us that the fear of rejection may shadow our lives, but it is only when we step out of that shadow that we truly shine. Embracing rejection as part of the journey allows us to grow, learn, and thrive in the face of adversity. Like our two friends, may you find the courage to dance to the beat of your own heart and discover the boundless possibilities that await when you unshackle yourself from the fear of rejection.

REJECTION & APPROVAL: THE SELF-ESTEEM LINK

A common thread between these two behaviors is low self-esteem, the very foundation that can exacerbate our dependence on external validation and deepen our fear of rejection. Here, we explore the connection between self-esteem and our inclination to seek approval or avoid rejection.

In the intricate dance of human emotions, rejection and approval often hold hands and waltz through our lives, affecting our self-esteem in profound ways. These two seemingly opposing forces share a fascinating link that intertwines their influence on how we perceive ourselves and navigate the world around us.

At the heart of this connection lies the foundation of self-esteem – the deeply rooted beliefs we hold about our own worth and value as individuals. Our self-esteem acts as a lens through which we interpret the world, shaping how we respond to both approval and rejection.

Let's delve into the self-esteem link between rejection and approval and uncover how this dynamic impacts our emotional well-being:

The Rejection-Seeking Paradox:

The need for approval and the fear of rejection are often two sides of the same coin. On one hand, we crave approval from others as validation of our worth. We seek external reassurance to bolster our self-esteem and validate our choices, actions, and decisions. This desire for approval can manifest in various ways, from seeking compliments to constantly seeking validation from others.

However, paradoxically, the intense need for approval can also lead us to fear rejection. The fear of being rejected or criticized by others can be so overwhelming that we may alter our behavior, thoughts, and even our true selves to avoid potential rejection. We become hyper-vigilant to any signs of disapproval, leading to a constant state of anxiety and apprehension.

Self-Esteem and Vulnerability:

At the heart of the rejection-approval link is vulnerability. When we seek approval, we are opening ourselves up to vulnerability by allowing others to influence our feelings of self-worth. Our self-esteem becomes contingent on the approval we receive, making us vulnerable to the opinions and judgments of others.

Conversely, the fear of rejection arises from the fear of being judged as unworthy or inadequate. We fear that rejection will confirm our deepest insecurities and weaknesses, further eroding our self-esteem. In this way, the fear of rejection acts as a defense mechanism, protecting us from potential emotional harm.

The Impact on Decision-Making:

The self-esteem link between rejection and approval profoundly affects our decision-making process. When our self-esteem is closely tied to external validation, we may make decisions based on what we believe will gain approval from others rather than staying true to our authentic selves. We may prioritize external expectations over our own desires and aspirations, leading to a loss of autonomy and personal fulfillment.

Moreover, the fear of rejection can paralyze us from taking risks and pursuing opportunities. The fear of failure and potential disapproval can deter us from stepping outside our comfort zones and exploring new possibilities. As a result, we may miss out on valuable experiences and personal growth.

Building Resilience and Authenticity:
To break free from the clutches of the rejection-approval link, we must cultivate resilience and authenticity. Resilience allows us to bounce back from rejection and setbacks, recognizing that rejection is a natural part of life and doesn't diminish our inherent worth. Authenticity empowers us to embrace our true selves and make decisions that align with our values and aspirations, rather than seeking external validation.

By nurturing a healthy sense of self-esteem that comes from within, we become less dependent on external approval and more immune to the fear of rejection. We can embrace vulnerability with courage, understanding that our self-worth doesn't depend on the acceptance or rejection of others.

In Conclusion:

In the complex interplay of emotions, rejection and approval are intertwined with the delicate thread of self-esteem. Recognizing and understanding this link is essential for fostering emotional well-being and personal growth. By building a strong foundation of self-esteem based on authenticity and resilience, we can liberate ourselves from the shackles of the rejection-approval paradox and live with a sense of freedom and self-empowerment.

SELF-ESTEEM: A TALE

In the enchanting village of Celestia, there lived a young girl named Seraphina. She was a bright, curious soul who had a heart full of dreams and ambitions. Seraphina's eyes sparkled with wonder as she gazed at the world around her, eager to explore and learn.

However, there was a little secret that Seraphina kept hidden from the world – she struggled with low self-esteem. Though she possessed extraordinary talents and a beautiful heart, she often doubted herself and felt unworthy of the love and admiration she received from her family and friends.

Every morning, as the sun painted the sky with hues of gold, Seraphina would look at herself in the mirror and whisper, "You're not good enough. You don't deserve all the wonderful things in your life." Those harsh words echoed in her mind, chipping away at her self-worth.

One day, while wandering through the forest, Seraphina stumbled upon a mysterious and ancient-looking book. Its leather cover was weathered with age, and its pages were filled with inscriptions that seemed to glow with a golden aura. The book was titled "The Mirror of Self-Esteem."

Intrigued, Seraphina opened the book and read its first page. It spoke of a magical mirror that could reflect one's true self – not just their physical appearance but also their innermost thoughts and feelings. Legend had it that gazing into this mirror would reveal the beauty and potential within, helping individuals embrace their uniqueness and build unshakeable self-esteem.

Guided by curiosity and a glimmer of hope, Seraphina embarked on a quest to find the Mirror of Self-Esteem. Along her journey, she encountered various challenges that tested her courage and determination. Each obstacle she overcame added a spark of confidence to her spirit, inching her closer to the mirror's location.

After days of adventure, Seraphina finally reached

the heart of the Enchanted Forest, where the Mirror of Self-Esteem was said to reside. It was a breathtaking sight – a magnificent mirror encased in a grand oak frame adorned with mystical symbols.

With trembling hands, Seraphina gazed into the mirror. At first, she saw her reflection as she had always perceived herself – filled with self-doubt and insecurities. But as she continued to look, a transformation began to occur. The mirror showed her moments of kindness, courage, and resilience – the times she had lifted others' spirits, stood up for what she believed in, and embraced her uniqueness.

With tears in her eyes, Seraphina realized that she was more than her doubts and fears. She was a tapestry of strengths and weaknesses, woven together to create a one-of-a-kind masterpiece. The mirror's magic revealed her true essence, and a newfound sense of self-esteem blossomed within her heart.

From that moment on, Seraphina carried the mirror's wisdom with her. Whenever self-doubt threatened to cloud her mind, she would look into the mirror and remind herself of her worth. The mirror became her constant companion, reflecting back the truth of her beautiful soul.

As word of Seraphina's transformation spread

throughout Celestia, other villagers started seeking the Mirror of Self-Esteem too. Seraphina, now confident in her own skin, guided them on their journeys of self-discovery. She encouraged them to embrace their imperfections, celebrate their uniqueness, and recognize their inherent worth.

The once timid and self-conscious Seraphina had become a beacon of light, illuminating the path to self-esteem for all who sought it. With each person she helped, her own self-esteem grew stronger, creating a beautiful cycle of empowerment and love.

And so, dear reader, the tale of Seraphina teaches us that self-esteem is not a destination to reach but a journey to embark upon. Like her, may you find the courage to seek your own Mirror of Self-Esteem and embrace the beautiful masterpiece that is you. Remember that you are worthy, you are loved, and you are enough – just as you are. Let your self-esteem be the guiding light that illuminates your path to a life filled with confidence, love, and boundless possibilities.

WHERE APPROVAL AND REJECTION COLLIDE

In this chapter, we unravel the intricate relationship between approval-seeking and rejection fear, unveiling how they can intensify one another, leading to emotional distress and self-doubt. Understanding this correlation is the key to breaking free from the cycle.

Where approval and rejection collide is the intersection where our deepest desires for validation and our intense fears of disapproval converge. It is the complex battleground of human emotions where seeking external approval clashes with the crippling fear of rejection, leading to a turbulent inner struggle that profoundly impacts our self-esteem and decision-making.

In this collision, we find ourselves trapped in a paradoxical dance. On one hand, we yearn for approval and validation from others, seeking their affirmation to validate our self-worth. We may constantly seek external validation, striving to meet the expectations and standards set by society or significant individuals in our lives. The desire for approval can drive us to seek compliments, bend ourselves to fit societal norms, and constantly seek reassurance from others.

On the other hand, lurking in the shadows is the fear of rejection. We dread the possibility of being judged, criticized, or excluded, as it threatens to shatter the fragile construct of our self-esteem. The fear of rejection can be so powerful that it stifles our authentic expression, silencing our true thoughts and emotions to avoid disapproval. It becomes a self-protective mechanism, shielding us from potential emotional pain and vulnerability.

The collision of approval and rejection creates a relentless tug-of-war within us. We may find ourselves in a constant quest for validation, yet paralyzed by the fear of rejection. We navigate life's choices with one eye on the approval of others and the other on avoiding any possible rejection.

This collision can have significant consequences in our lives. It may lead us to make decisions solely based on what we believe will gain approval from others, rather than following our own desires and passions. We may compromise our authenticity to fit into societal molds, losing touch with our true selves in the process. The fear of rejection can deter us from taking risks, pursuing opportunities, and embracing growth and change.

To navigate this tumultuous terrain, it is essential to cultivate a healthy sense of self-esteem that comes from within. By recognizing our inherent worth and embracing our authenticity, we can lessen the grip of external validation and become more resilient to the fear of rejection. Developing self-compassion and learning to accept ourselves, flaws and all, can provide us with the inner strength to navigate the complexities of seeking approval and facing rejection.

At the collision point of approval and rejection, there is an opportunity for growth and self-discovery. By embracing vulnerability and honoring our true selves, we can break free from the confines of seeking validation from others and find the courage to live authentically. In doing so, we liberate ourselves from the constraints of external judgments and nurture a sense of self-empowerment that transcends the need for approval or the fear of rejection.

APPROVAL: A TALE

Once upon a time in the whimsical town of Harmonyville, there lived two best friends named Adamu and Evian. They were known throughout the town for their incredible talents – Adamu was an exceptional painter, and Evian had a mesmerizing voice that could captivate even the most hardened hearts. Together, they dreamt of sharing their gifts with the world.

But there was one thing that held them back – their insatiable need for approval. Adamu would tirelessly seek validation from art critics, townsfolk, and even passerby who glanced at his paintings. Evian, on the other hand, constantly craved applause and adoration from her audience after every song she sang.

One sunny morning, as they sat on a wooden bench under the ancient oak tree, Adamu sighed and confessed, "Evian, I don't know why, but I can't paint without constantly worrying if people will like my work."

Evian nodded in understanding and replied, "Oh, Adamu, I feel the same way about my singing. It's as if my worth is tied to the number of applause I receive."

Their conversation was interrupted by the arrival of a curious traveler named Maestro Marcello. He was renowned for his wisdom and had traveled far and wide to share his insights with those in need.

Sensing their inner turmoil, Maestro Marcello approached Adamu and Evian with a knowing smile. "Ah, my dear friends, I couldn't help but overhear your conversation," he said kindly. "Seeking approval is a natural human desire, but relying on it entirely can stifle your creativity and imprison your true potential."

Both Adamu and Evian looked at him, eager to learn more. Maestro Marcello continued, "Imagine a world where artists painted not for the applause, but for the joy of creation. Where musicians sang not for the cheers, but to touch the hearts of listeners.

That, my friends, is where true artistry lies – in the uninhibited expression of your passion."

Adamu and Evian exchanged puzzled glances, uncertain of how to embrace this newfound wisdom. Sensing their confusion, Maestro Marcello shared a fable from his travels:

In a distant kingdom, there was a wise and eccentric king who held an annual arts festival. Artists from far and wide would showcase their work, and the winner would be granted a grand prize. The competition was fierce, and artists spent countless sleepless nights perfecting their masterpieces.

But there was one artist, a humble potter named Milo, who approached the festival differently. Milo didn't seek approval; he found solace in the soothing rhythm of his hands molding clay into beautiful forms. He didn't care if his pots were labeled "winning" or "ordinary." He simply enjoyed the process of creation.

When the festival day arrived, the kingdom was abuzz with excitement. As each artist displayed their work, the crowd marveled at their talent. But when it was Milo's turn, something magical happened – the audience fell silent.

Milo's pottery told a story of joy, love, and

authenticity. His creations touched the hearts of everyone present, leaving them in awe of his artistry. The eccentric king, moved by the depth of emotion in Milo's work, declared him the winner of the festival.

The moral of the fable was clear – true artistry lies not in seeking approval but in connecting with the emotions of the audience. Maestro Marcello looked at Adamu and Evian and said, "If you create from your heart, your art will resonate with others. Seek fulfillment in the act of creation itself, and approval will become a mere echo of your success."

Inspired by Maestro Marcello's words, Adamu and Evian decided to let go of their constant need for approval. They focused on the joy of expressing their talents, and something magical happened – their art flourished like never before. The townspeople could feel the passion and authenticity in their work, and their creations touched the souls of everyone who experienced them.

From that day on, Adamu and Evian painted and sang with a newfound sense of freedom and fulfillment. They were no longer bound by the opinions of others, and their art became a genuine reflection of their inner selves.

As their talents blossomed, so did their friendship. Together, they embraced the beauty of creating for the sheer joy of it, and their bond grew stronger than ever before. They learned that approval from others may come and go, but the truest form of approval was the love and acceptance they had for themselves and each other.

And so, Adamu and Evian's story serves as a timeless reminder that seeking approval from others can be a never-ending chase, but finding approval within yourself is the key to unlocking your true potential and setting your creativity free.

REJECTION: A TALE

In the quaint village of Willowbrook, there lived a young and ambitious inventor named Max. He was always tinkering with gadgets and contraptions, dreaming of creating something extraordinary that would leave a lasting impact on the world.

Max's enthusiasm and passion for inventing were contagious, and his family and friends admired his determination. However, there was one person in the village who never seemed impressed by Max's inventions – the stern and critical Mayor Wellington.

The Mayor was a traditionalist who believed that the village should stick to its old ways and shunned any change or innovation. Every time Max presented one of his inventions at the annual village fair, Mayor Wellington would scoff and dismiss it as foolish and unnecessary.

Despite the disapproval from the Mayor, Max refused to be discouraged. He continued to work tirelessly in his small workshop, fueled by the belief that one day, he would create something that would change minds and hearts.

One sunny afternoon, Max came up with his most ambitious invention yet – a flying machine that could carry people through the sky. He was certain that this creation would finally earn him the respect and approval he desired from the Mayor and the villagers.

With trembling excitement, Max unveiled his flying machine at the village fair. A crowd gathered around, curious to see what the young inventor had come up with this time. Max's heart pounded in his chest as he climbed into the cockpit and prepared for takeoff.

The moment of truth arrived, and Max activated the machine. To his delight, the contraption hummed to life, and the propellers whirred as it lifted off the ground. Gasps of awe filled the air as Max soared through the sky, the wind rushing through his hair.

However, his exhilaration was short-lived as he spotted Mayor Wellington standing in the distance, scowling and shaking his head in disapproval. Max's heart sank, and he felt a wave of rejection wash over him.

Feeling defeated and rejected, Max landed his flying machine and retreated to his workshop, questioning whether his dreams of inventing were worth pursuing anymore. He felt like an outsider in his own village, and the weight of the Mayor's disapproval weighed heavily on his shoulders.

But just as Max was on the brink of giving up, he received an unexpected visitor – a wise and eccentric inventor named Professor Alastair. Professor Alastair had heard about Max's flying machine and wanted to see it for himself.

Max hesitated, feeling unsure about showing his invention to yet another person who might reject it. However, the Professor's warm and encouraging smile put him at ease. The Professor studied the flying machine with genuine interest, asking thoughtful questions and offering valuable feedback.

As the two inventors talked, Max realized that rejection from one person didn't define his worth or the potential impact of his creations. Professor Alastair shared stories of his own rejections and how he learned to embrace them as stepping stones towards growth and improvement.

"You see, young Max," the Professor said, "rejection is a part of every inventor's journey. It's not the end of the road, but a chance to learn and evolve. Embrace your passion and continue to create, regardless of what others may say. Your inventions may not be for everyone, but they will find their way into the hearts of those who appreciate true innovation."

Feeling inspired and uplifted by the Professor's words, Max regained his confidence and determination. He realized that seeking approval from others was not the goal of his inventions – it was the joy of creation, the thrill of discovery, and the possibility of making a positive impact that mattered most.

Max returned to the village with renewed enthusiasm, ready to embrace rejection as a part of his journey as an inventor. He continued to invent with passion and perseverance, knowing that every rejection brought him one step closer to achieving his dreams.

Over time, Max's inventions began to win the hearts of the villagers, one by one. Mayor Wellington, too, couldn't help but be impressed by Max's resilience and creativity. Slowly but surely, he started to see the value of innovation and the positive changes it brought to the village.

In the end, Max's relentless pursuit of his dreams and his refusal to be defined by rejection transformed Willowbrook into a place where creativity and innovation flourished. His flying machine became a symbol of hope and inspiration for the entire village.

And so, Max's story teaches us that rejection is not a roadblock but a stepping stone on the path to success. Embrace it, learn from it, and let it fuel your passion for creating something extraordinary that leaves a lasting impact on the world.

REPAIRING YOUR SELF-ESTEEM

Empowerment begins with self-compassion and recognizing the origins of our validation-seeking tendencies. We'll delve into practical strategies to boost self-esteem, reclaiming control over our lives and nurturing a positive self-image.

Repairing your self-esteem is an essential and transformative journey of self-discovery and self-compassion. It involves recognizing and addressing the deep-rooted beliefs and thought patterns that have contributed to a negative self-image. By actively working to rebuild your self-esteem, you can regain your sense of worth, confidence, and agency over your life.

Self-Reflection:

The first step in repairing your self-esteem is self-reflection. Take the time to explore the origins of your low self-esteem and identify any past experiences, traumas, or negative messages that may have contributed to it. Understand that these beliefs may not be accurate reflections of who you truly are, but rather conditioned responses.

Self-Compassion:

Developing self-compassion is crucial in repairing your self-esteem. Be kind to yourself and recognize that everyone makes mistakes and faces challenges. Treat yourself with the same understanding and care that you would offer a dear friend in times of struggle.

Challenge Negative Thoughts:

Challenge and question the negative thoughts and beliefs that undermine your self-esteem. Replace them with more positive and affirming thoughts. Celebrate your strengths, accomplishments, and unique qualities.

Set Realistic Goals:

Set achievable and realistic goals for yourself. Break

down larger tasks into smaller, manageable steps, and celebrate each milestone you reach. Success in these goals will boost your confidence and sense of accomplishment.

Surround Yourself with Positivity:

Surround yourself with supportive and positive people who uplift and encourage you. Avoid toxic relationships that drain your self-esteem. Seek out those who value and appreciate you for who you are.

Cultivate Healthy Habits:

Take care of your physical and mental well-being. Engage in activities that bring you joy and fulfillment. Regular exercise, proper nutrition, and sufficient rest can positively impact your self-esteem.

Embrace Your Uniqueness:

Embrace your uniqueness and individuality. Recognize that you are a valuable and worthy person, irrespective of external validations or comparisons to others. Accept and celebrate your authentic self.

Practice Mindfulness:

Practicing mindfulness can help you become more aware of your thoughts and feelings in the present moment without judgment. This awareness allows you to respond to challenges and setbacks with greater clarity and self-compassion.

Seek Professional Support:

If repairing your self-esteem feels overwhelming or challenging, don't hesitate to seek professional support from a therapist or counselor. They can provide guidance and tools tailored to your specific needs.

Be Patient and Persistent:

Repairing your self-esteem is a process that takes time and effort. Be patient with yourself and acknowledge that it may not happen overnight. Stay persistent in your commitment to cultivating a positive self-image.

By actively engaging in these steps and embracing self-compassion and self-acceptance, you can repair your self-esteem and foster a greater sense of self-worth and self-confidence. Remember that you are deserving of love, respect, and validation – starting with the love and respect you give to yourself.

TAKING BACK - "CONTROL"

To overcome the fear of rejection and approval-seeking, we must regain autonomy and agency in our lives. Learn how small changes and stepping outside our comfort zones can help us feel more in control and capable of tackling life's challenges.

Taking back control refers to the empowering process of reclaiming authority and autonomy over your life, decisions, and actions. It involves breaking free from external influences, limiting beliefs, and unhealthy patterns that have been holding you back. By taking back control, you become the driver of your life's journey, shaping it according to your desires, values, and aspirations.

Identifying External Influences:

The first step in taking back control is recognizing the external factors that have been influencing your decisions and actions. This may include seeking approval from others, conforming to societal expectations, or succumbing to peer pressure. Acknowledging these influences is essential to understand how they have impacted your choices.

Understanding Limiting Beliefs:

Limiting beliefs are negative thought patterns that undermine your self-confidence and potential. These beliefs may be rooted in past experiences or ingrained from childhood. By identifying and challenging these beliefs, you can break free from self-imposed limitations and embrace a more positive mindset.

Setting Boundaries:

Taking back control often involves setting healthy boundaries with others. This means knowing your limits and asserting your needs and preferences without feeling guilty or obligated to please everyone. Setting boundaries helps create a balanced and respectful dynamic in your relationships.

Embracing Decision-Making:

Empower yourself by embracing decision-making. Avoid procrastination and indecisiveness by making choices that align with your values and long-term goals. Embrace the idea that even mistakes are opportunities for growth and learning.

Focusing on Personal Growth:

Taking back control includes a commitment to personal growth and self-improvement. Continuously strive to enhance your skills, knowledge, and emotional intelligence. Embrace challenges and view them as opportunities to evolve and become a stronger individual.

Practicing Self-Reflection:

Engage in regular self-reflection to gain insights into your thoughts, emotions, and behaviors. Self-awareness helps you understand your motivations and triggers, enabling you to respond to situations more consciously and effectively.

Embracing Resilience:

Life is filled with uncertainties and challenges. Taking back control involves cultivating resilience and adaptability. Embrace setbacks as a natural part of life and develop the ability to bounce back stronger after difficult times.

Letting Go of Perfectionism:

Striving for perfection can be paralyzing and prevent you from taking action. Embrace imperfections as part of the human experience and focus on progress rather than perfection. Celebrate your achievements, no matter how small.

Surrounding Yourself with Positivity:

Surround yourself with positive influences and supportive individuals who uplift and inspire you. Distance yourself from toxic relationships or environments that drain your energy and hinder your progress.

Celebrating Your Successes:

Taking back control involves celebrating your successes, no matter how big or small. Acknowledge your accomplishments and recognize the efforts you have made to reclaim your power and live life on your terms.

Taking back control is a transformative journey that empowers you to step into your true potential and live authentically. It requires courage, self-compassion, and a willingness to challenge old beliefs and habits. By doing so, you create a life that reflects your values, passions, and aspirations, ultimately leading to greater fulfillment and happiness.

CONTROL: A TALE

Once upon a time in the bustling city of Metroville, there lived a young woman named Emma. Emma was ambitious, driven, and had a deep desire to take control of her life. She had always been someone who believed in the power of personal agency and taking charge of her destiny.

Emma worked as a talented marketing executive at a prominent advertising agency. She loved her job and was exceptional at what she did. However, she couldn't shake the feeling that she was capable of even more. She yearned to start her own marketing firm and be her own boss, but fear and self-doubt held her back.

One day, as she was sitting in her office, she received a surprise email from an old college friend, Mark. Mark had recently started his own successful tech company and wanted to catch up with Emma over lunch.

Excited to see Mark again, Emma agreed to the meeting. As they chatted over lunch, Mark noticed the spark in Emma's eyes whenever she talked about her passion for marketing. He asked her why she hadn't started her own firm yet, and Emma admitted that she was afraid of the risks and uncertainties that came with being an entrepreneur.

Mark leaned in and said, "Emma, I know exactly what you're going through. When I first started my company, I had the same fears and doubts. But you know what? Taking control of my life and following my dreams was the best decision I ever made."

He continued, "Life is too short to be stuck in a place of comfort and security. If you have a passion and a vision, you owe it to yourself to pursue it. You have the talent, the skills, and the drive to make it happen. You just need to believe in yourself and take that first step."

Emma listened to Mark's words and felt a surge of inspiration. She realized that she had been allowing fear to hold her back from reaching her full potential. She had been waiting for the perfect moment, but Mark's story made her realize that there would never be a perfect time to take a risk.

With newfound determination, Emma decided to take control of her life and follow her dreams. She spent countless hours creating a business plan, networking with potential clients, and building her brand. It wasn't easy, and there were moments of doubt along the way, but Emma refused to let anything stop her.

Finally, the day came when Emma launched her own marketing firm, "Embrace Marketing Solutions." The excitement and sense of accomplishment she felt were unparalleled. She was now in charge of her destiny, and it was a liberating feeling.

As Emma's business grew, so did her confidence. She proved herself as a force to be reckoned with in the marketing world, and clients flocked to her for her innovative ideas and impeccable execution.

With each success, Emma became more aware of the incredible power that comes with taking control of one's life. She no longer waited for opportunities to come her way; she created them herself. She was no longer held back by fear of failure; she saw failure as a valuable learning experience.

As word of Emma's success spread, she became an inspiration to others. Young professionals and aspiring entrepreneurs sought her advice and mentorship. Emma was more than happy to share her story and encourage others to take charge of their lives, just like she did.

In the end, Emma's journey to taking control and being in charge was a testament to the power of self-belief and determination. She proved that when you are willing to step out of your comfort zone and embrace the unknown, amazing things can happen.

And so, Emma's story teaches us that we all have the ability to take control of our lives and shape our destinies. It may be scary, and there may be challenges along the way, but the rewards are well worth it. So, don't be afraid to take that leap of faith and be in charge of your own life. Your dreams are waiting for you to make them a reality.

REFRAMING REJECTION AND APPROVAL

In this chapter, we challenge the conventional perception of rejection and approval, encouraging a healthy perspective on both. Embracing rejection as an opportunity for growth and discerning between healthy and unhealthy approval is vital for our emotional well-being.

Reframing rejection and approval involves shifting our perspectives and changing the way we perceive these two concepts. Instead of viewing them as purely negative or positive, we learn to see them in a more balanced and empowering light. By reframing rejection and approval, we can cultivate healthier self-esteem and make more authentic choices in our lives.

Embracing Rejection as Growth:

Instead of fearing rejection, we can reframe it as a natural part of life's journey. Rejection is not a reflection of our worth, but rather an opportunity for growth and learning. Each rejection can provide valuable insights and help us improve ourselves or our approach in the future.

Valuing Self-Approval:

While seeking approval from others can be validating, true empowerment comes from self-approval. Reframe approval as a positive reinforcement, but not the sole determinant of your self-worth. Trust in your own judgment and decisions, and recognize that you have the power to validate yourself.

Recognizing Healthy and Unhealthy Approval:

Distinguish between healthy approval and unhealthy validation-seeking. Healthy approval comes from genuine support, encouragement, and recognition from those who genuinely care for your well-being. Unhealthy validation-seeking, on the other hand, involves compromising your values and authenticity to gain acceptance from others.

Celebrating Independence:

Reframe the need for approval as an opportunity to celebrate your independence and uniqueness. Embrace your individuality, and recognize that seeking approval from others should not compromise your sense of self.

Acknowledging the Role of Feedback:

Approval and rejection can both be forms of feedback. Embrace feedback as an essential aspect of personal and professional growth. Constructive feedback can help us improve and make better choices, while unwarranted approval may not always lead us in the right direction.

Focusing on Intrinsic Motivation:

Instead of seeking approval externally, focus on intrinsic motivation—doing things because they align with your values, passions, and purpose. When your actions are driven by genuine passion and enthusiasm, external validation becomes less significant.

Letting Go of Perfectionism:

Reframe approval-seeking tendencies that stem from perfectionism. Embrace the idea that you are allowed to make mistakes and learn from them. Perfection is an unrealistic standard, and embracing imperfection allows for more authentic and fulfilling experiences.

Emphasizing Self-Compassion:

Cultivate self-compassion when facing rejection or seeking approval. Treat yourself with kindness and understanding, just as you would support a friend going through a similar experience. Remember that everyone experiences rejection at some point, and it does not define your worth.

Focusing on Alignment:

Instead of seeking approval from others, focus on alignment with your own values, goals, and passions. When your choices align with your authentic self, you naturally attract supportive people and experiences that resonate with your journey.

Celebrating Resilience:

Reframe rejection as an opportunity to showcase

resilience and determination. Each rejection you overcome strengthens your emotional resilience and fortitude. Celebrate your ability to bounce back from setbacks and continue pursuing your dreams.

By reframing rejection and approval, we liberate ourselves from the burdens of external validation and rejection sensitivity. Embracing a more balanced perspective empowers us to lead more authentic and fulfilling lives, free from the constraints of seeking constant approval from others. Ultimately, our self-esteem becomes rooted in self-acceptance and self-validation, leading to a greater sense of fulfillment and self-empowerment.

EMBRACING EMPOWERMENT

As we conclude our journey, we celebrate the empowering transformation from seeking validation to self-approval. Understanding the interconnectedness of seeking approval and fearing rejection empowers us to navigate life's challenges with newfound strength and resilience.

In a world that constantly bombards us with messages and expectations, embracing empowerment can be a transformative and liberating choice. Empowerment is not just a buzzword; it's a powerful concept that holds the potential to positively impact every aspect of our lives. When we choose to embrace empowerment, we open ourselves up to a wealth of advantages that can lead to personal growth, fulfillment, and a sense of purpose.

Let's explore some of the key advantages of embracing empowerment:

Self-Confidence:

Embracing empowerment fosters self-confidence. When we believe in our abilities and trust our judgment, we are more willing to take risks and pursue our goals without fear of failure or rejection. Self-confidence allows us to face challenges head-on and view setbacks as opportunities for growth.

Autonomy and Independence:

Empowerment liberates us from the need for constant external validation. It encourages us to make decisions based on our own values, desires, and aspirations. By being self-reliant and independent, we take control of our lives and chart our own paths.

Resilience:

Embracing empowerment builds emotional resilience. It equips us with the inner strength and adaptability to bounce back from adversity and face life's obstacles with determination. Resilience allows us to navigate through tough times and come out stronger on the other side.

Personal Growth:
Empowerment fuels personal growth and continuous self-improvement. When we are empowered, we actively seek opportunities for learning and development. We embrace challenges as stepping stones for progress and are open to trying new experiences that expand our horizons.

Positive Mindset:
Empowerment nurtures a positive mindset. It shifts our focus from dwelling on limitations to embracing possibilities. A positive outlook enhances our overall well-being, fosters creativity, and enables us to find solutions even in the face of difficulties.

Setting Boundaries:
Embracing empowerment enables us to set healthy boundaries in our relationships and work-life. We become assertive in expressing our needs and desires, ensuring that our time and energy are directed toward what truly matters to us.

Decision-Making:
Empowerment empowers us to make well-informed decisions. By tapping into our inner wisdom and

values, we can make choices that align with our long-term vision, bringing us closer to achieving our goals.

Sense of Purpose:

Embracing empowerment helps us discover and live in alignment with our purpose. We gain clarity about our passions and the impact we want to make in the world. This sense of purpose gives our actions greater meaning and fulfillment.

Leadership:

Empowerment breeds leadership qualities. When we empower ourselves, we are more likely to inspire and empower others. As leaders, we encourage those around us to embrace their potential and contribute positively to their communities.

Health and Well-Being:

Embracing empowerment positively impacts our overall health and well-being. It reduces stress and anxiety levels, as we feel more in control of our lives. It promotes a harmonious balance between our mental, emotional, and physical selves.

Effecting Change:

Empowerment enables us to be catalysts for positive change in our lives and communities. When we recognize our own power, we can work collectively to address societal issues and create a more inclusive and equitable world.

In conclusion, embracing empowerment is not just about a fleeting moment of inspiration; it's about adopting a mindset and lifestyle that can lead to profound advantages. It's a journey of self-discovery, resilience, and growth. By embracing empowerment, we can break free from limitations, embrace our authentic selves, and make a meaningful impact in the world.

So, why wait?

Take the first step on this empowering journey and unlock your true potential.

EPILOGUE

With the wisdom gained from this book, readers embark on a life free from the shackles of approval-seeking and rejection fear. Embracing their true selves, they embark on a journey of self-empowerment, compassion, and inner strength, ready to face life's uncertainties with courage and grace.

ACKNOWLEDGEMENT

Writing a book is never a solitary endeavor, and I am humbled and grateful for the support and encouragement I have received throughout this journey. I would like to express my deepest appreciation to the following individuals and groups:

To the members of The SURGE Community, thank you for your unwavering support and inspiration. Your enthusiasm and engagement have been instrumental in shaping the ideas and concepts in this book.

To Glory Ivharue, the most influential woman in my life, thank you for your guidance, encouragement, and belief in my abilities. Your unwavering support has been a driving force behind this project.

To my friends and family, thank you for understanding and supporting me during the countless hours I spent writing and revising this book. Your love and encouragement kept me motivated even during the most challenging times.

To my readers, thank you for embarking on this journey with me. Your interest and curiosity in the topics explored in this book are what make the effort worthwhile.

And finally, to myself, Oreoluwa, I acknowledge the courage and dedication it took to bring this book to life. May this be a reminder to always stay true to my passions and continue striving for personal growth.

With heartfelt gratitude,

Oreoluwa.

ABOUT THE AUTHOR

Oreoluwa O. Olaleye

 Oreoluwa is a passionate writer, philosopher, and advocate for self-empowerment. With a profound understanding of emotions and logic, he explores the intricate human experience through his words. In his twenties, Oreoluwa has gained valuable life experiences that have shaped his perspective on seeking approval and overcoming rejection. As an author, his works aim to inspire others to embrace their true selves, break free from external validation, and cultivate inner strength. With a unique blend of wisdom and humor, Oreoluwa's writing engages readers in meaningful introspection and empowers them to lead fulfilling lives. When he's not writing, Oreoluwa enjoys exploring the realms of music, fashion, and creativity.

BOOKS BY THIS AUTHOR

The Adventures Of Tito And Maya

Join Tito, a friendly fairy, and Maya, a mischievous pixie, as they embark on delightful adventures in their enchanted forest home. Together, they learn valuable life lessons, make new friends, and spread happiness through their magical world.

The Mischievous Adventures Of Giggle And Grin

Giggle and Grin are two playful and mischievous twins who live in a world where laughter is the most potent magic. Follow their hilarious escapades as they spread joy and laughter wherever they go, teaching everyone the importance of finding humor in life's ups and downs.

Her View: Guided By Emotions, Against

Logic; For Humanity.

With a keen focus on compassion, empathy, and authenticity, "Her View" delves into the multifaceted experiences of women as they navigate the complexities of life. From personal relationships to societal contributions, this book showcases how emotions can be a powerful force for positive change and human connection.

Seduction: ...An Intricate Story Of Lust.

A gripping tale of passion, desire, and uncertainty. Follow the tumultuous journey of characters entangled in a web of seductive allure and perplexing emotions, as they grapple with the complexities of love and the blurred lines between attraction and confusion.

Confusion: Lost, Uncertain And Disoriented.

Whether facing personal dilemmas, existential questions, or the complexities of a changing world, "Confusion" serves as a guide to navigate the uncertain terrain with courage, gaining clarity and wisdom along the way. Prepare to embark on a captivating journey of introspection and emerge with a deeper understanding of the power and potential hidden within moments of bewilderment.

The Gemini Effect

The Gemini Effect: Takes readers on a thought-provoking exploration of the complexities surrounding Donald Trump's persona and its profound impact on the United States. The book highlights the contrasting qualities that defined Trump, including his charismatic showmanship and unyielding determination as a businessman. It delves into how his dual nature influenced his political style, communication strategies, and policy decisions during his presidency. While focusing on Trump, the book also prompts a broader examination of the dynamics and challenges inherent in political leadership. It emphasizes the interconnectedness between leaders and their societies and encourages readers to consider the inspiring and divisive potential of dualistic leaders. Ultimately, "The Gemini Effect" aims to stimulate dialogue, critical thinking, and a deeper understanding of leadership's multifaceted nature, appealing to those interested in Trump's persona, political power dynamics, and the shaping forces of nations.

Clarity: Clear, Focused And Certain.

Drawing from a wealth of wisdom and real-life stories, this transformative read delves into the profound power of clarity and its ability to illuminate every facet of our existence. Through introspective reflections and practical guidance, readers will navigate the complexities of their inner world, shedding light on hidden passions, values, and aspirations. From decision-making to relationships, "Clarity" empowers readers to make mindful choices and forge authentic connections. With each page, embark on a journey of self-discovery, unraveling the layers of uncertainty to reveal a life of purpose and direction. Embrace the transformative gift of clarity and unlock the boundless potential that lies within, guiding you towards a life of meaning and profound fulfillment.

Tangled: A Bit Of Confusion.

"Tangled" is a poignant tale of love, betrayal, and the intricate complexities of family bonds. Follow the lives of Titi, Tutu, and Tana as they navigate the tumultuous journey of love and heartbreak, torn between loyalty to each other and the weight of their own desires. Can their sisterly bond withstand the trials that fate has laid before them, or will the revelations of their shared past lead to irreversible consequences? In this tale of shattered illusions and hidden truths, the Owolabi family will learn that sometimes, love's journey takes unforeseen turns, leaving their hearts forever entangled in a delicate dance of hope and despair.

The Right Person: #30 Profound Questions; To Be Sure You're Making The Right Decision.

Discover how to distinguish genuine love from infatuation, nurture emotional intimacy, and build a foundation of trust and commitment. Through personal anecdotes, practical advice, and reflective insights, Oreoluwa sheds light on the beauty of being with the right person and the impact it has on your overall happiness and fulfillment.

Debt$: The Subtle Art Of Borrowing To Be Rich

"The Subtle ART of Borrowing to be Rich" is not just a mere collection of tips and strategies; it is a profound exploration of the borrower's mindset, challenging conventional beliefs and paving the way for a transformational approach to finances. With wit and wisdom, the author imparts invaluable lessons on leveraging credit wisely, navigating the borrower-lender relationship, and fostering a wealth-oriented mindset.

www.ingramcontent.com/pod-product-compliance
Lightning Source LLC
Chambersburg PA
CBHW070955250726
48663CB00002B/232